Contents

From MY HEART to YOURS

I am so excited that you have chosen to be part of a *Life's Healing Choices Small Group Study*! Before you begin, I would like to share with you the purpose of a *Life's Healing Choices Small Group Study*, the Small Group Guidelines, and the Covenant that has been put in place to ensure your safety as you share!

LIFE'S HEALING CHOICES SMALL GROUP PURPOSE STATEMENT

Life's Healing Choices Small Group Study is an eight-week study that is designed to help you start to discover and face your hurts, hang-ups, and habits for perhaps the first time in your life. It is my prayer and goal that as the weeks pass, you will begin to find God's hope and healing. In addition, God will lead you to help others begin to make positive and healthy choices.

Remember that our hurts, hang-ups, and habits did not

occur overnight. Many of us have lived with our poor choices for years. We cannot expect to be completely free from them in only eight weeks. This small group is your courageous beginning of finding freedom from your life's hurts, hang-ups, and habits!

Your small group will provide you with a great understanding and working knowledge of each of the eight Healing Choices and why it is so important to complete them *in order and at your own speed.*

Your *Life's Healing Choices* small group is *not* designed for you to actually complete each choice in one week. Some choices will take much longer than others to finish. However, answering and discussing the questions found in each weekly lesson will help you, when you are ready, to complete the "Make the Choice" sections found at the end of each chapter of *Life's Healing Choices.* That is why you must find someone, outside of your small group time, who is a safe person with whom you can share your healing journey.

LIFE'S HEALING CHOICES SMALL GROUP GUIDELINES AND THE SMALL GROUP COVENANT

Your *Life's Healing Choices* small group needs to be a safe place if it is going to be successful and fulfilling. The *Life's Healing Choices* Small Group Guidelines and the Small Group Covenant ensure that your small group will be a safe place for you to share!

The following are the *Life's Healing Choices* Small Group Guidelines. They should be read at the beginning of every meeting:

LIFE'S HEALING CHOICES SMALL GROUP GUIDELINES

1. Keep your sharing focused on your own thoughts and feelings.

2. Each person is free to express feelings without interruption.

3. We are here to support one another. We will not attempt to fix one another.

4. Anonymity and confidentiality are basic requirements. What is shared in the group stays in the group! The only exception is when someone threatens to harm themselves or others.

5. All *Life's Healing Choices* small groups are same-sex groups!

LIFE'S HEALING CHOICES SMALL GROUP COVENANT

The *Life's Healing Choices* Small Group Study Covenant is extremely important for two reasons:

1. It helps to ensure that your group is safe for individuals to share their hurts, hang-ups, and habits.

2. It helps each member of the group keep their commitment to complete all eight weeks of the small group.

Let's take a look at the covenant line by line.

I will make attending all eight weeks of my *Life's Healing Choices* group a priority. I will come to the meeting prepared.
I will have written out my responses to each of the lesson's questions.

Matthew 5:37 (NIV) tells us, *"Simply let your 'Yes' be 'Yes,' and your 'No,' 'No'; anything beyond this comes from the evil one."* It is important that you attend all eight weeks of the *Life's Healing Choices* small group meetings. If you miss one week you will miss a lot. Each week new material and learning is introduced. Each lesson builds on the last. It is also important for you to complete each weekly assignment prior to the scheduled meeting.

I will pray daily for each of the individuals in my group.

James 5:16 (NIV) tells us, *"Therefore confess your sins to each other and pray for each other so that you may be healed. The prayer of a righteous man is powerful and effective."* Prayer is so important to the success of your *Life's Healing Choices* group. In fact, your group will not succeed without it. Prayer should not only be a major part of every meeting, but as a group you should agree to hold each other in prayer throughout the week. Your small group time will end with a time of prayer requests and prayer. There is a "Prayer Requests" page at the end of each week's lesson.

I will keep my group safe by following the *Life's Healing Choices* Small Group Guidelines.

In Matthew 22:39 (NIV) Jesus commands us, *"Love your neighbor as yourself."* The *Life's Healing Choices* Small Group

Guidelines are really expressions of love and respect for the other individuals in your group. You desire your *Life's Healing Choices* small group to be a safe place for you. Therefore, the other group members deserve the same respect from you. The five guidelines help keep the group safe for everyone. They are not there to discourage participation but to enhance it! It is the responsibility of each participant to follow the five guidelines.

I will get additional help with my hurts, hang-ups, and habits if needed.

In Proverbs 20:5 (KJV) we are told, "*Counsel in the heart of man is like deep water; but a man of understanding will draw it out.*" Each small group member needs to be fully aware that their hurts, hang-ups, and habits may require additional help. The hurts, hang-ups, and habits that you may discover through completing this eight-week small group study may be overwhelming to you. There is nothing wrong with seeking and getting additional help. It is making a "Healing Choice." God has provided many resources to help you in your time of need. You can start attending a Celebrate Recovery meeting at a church near you. To find the nearest location go to www.celebraterecovery.com. You can also contact your pastor or a Christian counselor.

I will ask one member, of the same sex, in my group to be my accountability partner.

In Ecclesiastes 4:9–10 (NIV) we are told, "*Two are better than one, because they have a good return for their work: If one falls down, his friend can help him up. But pity the man who falls and has no one to help him up!*" Accountability is essential to successfully completing the *Life's Healing Choices* Small Group Study.

An individual should not attempt to take this journey alone. The words "one another" appear in the New Testament over fifty times. We need others, those we determine are "safe," to come alongside us as we complete *Life's Healing Choices*. We need to agree to allow them to confront us in love and for us to be able to give them the same gift in return. We need someone we can talk to during the week if we get stuck on a certain question or are going through a difficult time.

The *Life's Healing Choices* Small Group Covenant, on the next page, should be signed by you and your group facilitator at the beginning of your first small group meeting.

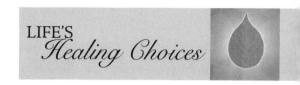

SMALL GROUP COVENANT

I commit to the following:

+ I will make attending all eight weeks of my *Life's Healing Choices* group a priority. I will come to the meetings prepared. I will have written out my responses to each of the lesson's questions. Matthew 5:37

+ I will pray daily for each of the individuals in my group. James 5:16

+ I will keep my group safe by following the *Life's Healing Choices* Small Group Guidelines. Matthew 22:39

+ I will get additional help with my hurts, hang-ups, and habits if needed. Proverbs 20:5

+ I will ask one member, of the same sex, in my group to be my accountability partner. Ecclesiastes 4:9–10

Signed _____ Date _____

Life's Healing Choices Small Group Participant

Signed _____ Date _____

Life's Healing Choices Small Group Facilitator

7

LET'S GET STARTED!

Now you understand the purpose of a *Life's Healing Choices* small group and the Guidelines and you have signed the Covenant. You are ready to get started!

You are in my prayers. May God bless you and protect you as you take this courageous step!

John Baker

> **Important Note to *Life's Healing Choices* Small Group Facilitators:** Please read "How to Facilitate a *Life's Healing Choices* Small Group" in the appendix, page 122. You will find important information on how to get your small group started and keep it on track.

Realize I'm not God.

I *admit* that I am powerless to control
my tendency to do the wrong thing
and that my life is unmanageable.

R
E
C
O
V
E
R
Y

"Happy are those who know they are spiritually poor."
Matthew 5:3 TEV

Admitting NEED

The REALITY Choice

THE REALITY CHOICE PRAYER

Dear God, I want to take the first choice to healing and spiritual health today. I realize I am not You, God. I've often tried to control my problems, my pain, my image, and even other people—as if I were You. I'm sorry. I've tried to deny my problems by staying busy and keeping myself distracted. But I'm not running anymore. I admit that I am helpless to control this tendency to do things I know are unhealthy for me. Today I am asking for Your help. I humbly ask You to take all the pieces of my unmanageable life and begin the process of healing. Please heal me. Please give me the strength to choose health. Help me stick with this process for the next seven choices. In Your name, I pray. Amen.

WEEK 1 ASSIGNMENTS

1. Read *Life's Healing Choices*—Introduction (pages 1–10).

2. Read *Life's Healing Choices*—Choice 1 (pages 13–35).

3. Complete the *Small Group Study* questions for Choice 1. Be specific!

Important reminder: Please come to your small group prepared. That means completing both the reading and written assignments prior to your weekly meeting!

You may not have enough room to complete the answers in the space provided. Don't let that stop you; just use a notebook or journal.

The *Life's Healing Choices* Small Group Covenant, on page 7, should be signed by you and your small group facilitator at the beginning of your first small group meeting.

Choice 1

SMALL GROUP STUDY QUESTIONS

Part of our human nature is to refuse change until our pain exceeds our fear—fear of change, that is. We simply deny the pain until it gets so bad that we are crushed and finally realize we need some help. Why don't we save ourselves a bit of misery and admit *now* what we're inevitably going to have to admit later? *We are not God,* and we desperately need God because our lives are unmanageable without Him. We'll be forced to learn that lesson someday. We may as well admit it now.

THE CAUSE OF OUR PROBLEMS

On page 14 of *Life's Healing Choices,* we look at the *cause of our problems.* There are three major causes.

1. Our Tendency to Do Wrong

Romans 7:15–17 NLT tells us, "*I don't understand myself at all, for I really want to do what is right, but I don't do it. Instead, I do the very thing I hate. I know perfectly well that what I am doing is wrong . . . but I can't help myself, because it is sin inside me that makes me do these evil things.*"

+ What do these verses mean to you?

+ How do they apply to your own life?

+ List some specific examples.

2. Our Desire to Be God

We want to decide for ourselves what is right and what is wrong. In essence, we want to be God. But this is nothing new. Trying to be God is humankind's oldest problem (read Genesis, chapter 3).

+ Why do we continue making poor choices?

+ Why do we desire to be in control?

3. Our Attempts to Play God

We play God by trying to control our image, other people, our problems, and our pain.

+ List some ways we try to control our image.

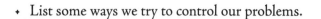

+ List some ways we try to control our problems.

+ List some ways we try to control our pain.

THE CURE FOR OUR PROBLEMS

On page 20 of *Life's Healing Choices*, we look at the *cure for our problems*. The cure for our problems comes in a strange form: it comes through admitting weakness and through a humble heart. The beatitude for Choice 1 is:

> *"Happy are those who know they are spiritually poor."*
> MATTHEW 5:3 TEV

Making the first choice to healing means acknowledging that we are not God. Doing so means recognizing and admitting three important facts of life:

1. I admit that I am powerless to change my past.

+ What does that fact mean to you?

2. I admit that I am powerless to control other people.

+ What does that fact mean to you?

3. I admit that I am powerless to cope with my harmful habits, behaviors, and actions.

+ What does that fact mean to you?

Starting on page 27 of *Life's Healing Choices,* you will find Elaine's and Joe's Stories of Changed Lives for Choice 1.

1. List some specific examples of the *causes* of Elaine's and Joe's problems.

   + Elaine:

   + Joe:

2. List some specific examples of the actions Elaine and Joe took to find the *cure* for their problems.

   + Elaine:

   + Joe:

3. If you feel safe, share the hurt, hang-up, or habit you are
    dealing with today.

Important reminder: The wise writer of Ecclesiastes said, *"Two
are better than one, because they have a good return for their work: If
one falls down, his friend can help him up. But pity the man who falls
and has no one to help him up! . . . Though one may be overpowered,
two can defend themselves. A cord of three strands is not quickly
broken"* (4:9–10, 12 NIV).

The next few chapters of *Life's Healing Choices* will guide
you in choosing this person. You'll be looking for someone
you can honestly and openly talk to. This person needs to be
nonjudgmental and someone with whom you can safely share
your personal journal notes. This person should be willing to
share his or her life and struggles with you as well. Once God
shows you that safe person, set up a meeting time and ask him or
her to join with you in this recovery journey toward healing by
being your accountability partner. This person may be someone
in your small group, a relative, a friend, a neighbor, a coworker, or
someone in your church family.

Be sure the person you choose is of the same sex. You will be
sharing very personal details of your life as you go through each

of the Healing Choices. Some of the issues will be inappropriate to share with someone of the opposite sex.

As you work through the next few chapters, if you cannot find a safe person to share with, visit www.celebraterecovery.com to locate a Celebrate Recovery group near you. There you will find people who have worked through the eight choices and who will be glad to help and support you as you begin your healing journey. Just remember, this journey should not be traveled alone. You need others to listen to you, encourage you, support you, and demonstrate God's love to you.

Notes

FOR CHOICE 1

LIFE'S
Healing Choices
SMALL GROUP STUDY

Prayer Requests
FOR WEEK 1

R

Earnestly believe that God exists,

that I *matter* to Him, and that He

has the power to help me recover.

C
O
V
E
R
Y

"Happy are those who mourn, for they shall be comforted."
MATTHEW 5:4 TEV/NIV

Getting HELP

The HOPE Choice

THE HOPE CHOICE PRAYER

Dear God, please help me not to ignore this pain You are using to alert me to my need for help. In the past, as I've ignored the denial busters You've allowed in my life, I have actually refused Your help. I am so sorry for this and ask Your help in facing the truth and trusting You to care for me. You know and care about all the pain and hurt I have in my life. Today I need Your help. I can't do it on my own. I have tried, and I keep coming up empty.

First, I pray for Your power in my life. I need Your power to break habits I can't break. I need Your power to help me do the things that I know are right but can't seem to do on my own. I need Your power to break free from my past. I ask for Your power to get on with the plans You have for my life.

Next, I pray for love. I want real love. I want to be able to love people and have them love me. I pray that with Your love I can let go of past hurts and failures so I can tear down the walls of fake intimacy. God, I ask You to help me have genuine intimacy with You and others. Help me not be afraid of really loving and of really being loved.

I also pray for real self-control. I realize that I'm really not in control until I allow Christ to be in control of my life and circumstances.

God, please grant me Your power, love, and self-control. Help me to continue making Healing Choices. Amen.

WEEK 2 ASSIGNMENTS

1. Read *Life's Healing Choices*—Choice 1 (pages 37–69).

2. Complete the *Small Group Study* questions for Choice 2. Be specific!

Important reminder: Please come to your small group prepared. That means completing both the reading and written assignments prior to your weekly meeting!

Choice 2

SMALL GROUP STUDY QUESTIONS

In the first choice, we learned that no matter how hard we try to keep everything under control, we are powerless to control our tendency to do wrong and that our lives are unmanageable. In this choice we'll begin moving out of the role of playing God and into the role of receiving God's power. We will also gain a vision of the hope and help God offers us. But first, we'll look at two of God's blessings in disguise: grief and pain—and when we do, we'll learn how to tap into God's power.

GOD'S PATHWAY TO COMFORT

On page 38 of *Life's Healing Choices*, we learned that grief is God's pathway to comfort. We mourn over our past mistakes, and we even mourn over our loss of control. In the end, God leads us to His comfort, if we will just trust in Him. As the beatitude for this choice says,

> *"Happy are those who mourn, for they shall be comforted."*
> MATTHEW 5:4 TEV/NIV

+ How can mourning over our past mistakes and our loss of control lead us to comfort? Be specific and share some examples of how this has happened in your own life.

As long as we don't get stuck in the mourning process, mourning can serve as the pathway to the comfort and to the help and hope God has ready for us. The same promise God gave His people of old, He gives us today: *"To all who mourn in Israel, he will give beauty for ashes, joy instead of mourning, praise instead of despair. For the Lord has planted them like strong and graceful oaks for his own glory"* (Isaiah 61:3 NLT).

+ In your own words, what does Isaiah 61:3 mean to you? Especially focus on *"he will give beauty for ashes, joy instead of mourning, praise instead of despair."*

GOD'S ANTIDOTE FOR DENIAL

On page 39 of *Life's Healing Choices*, we also learn that pain is God's antidote for denial. To deny our pain is to refuse

God's power to help us recover. One man said, "The acid of my pain finally ate through the wall of my denial." God uses three denial busters to get our attention, to force us to move into recovery and away from the choices and circumstances that have messed up our lives. They are *crisis, confrontation, and catastrophe.*

- How has, or is, God using one of the three denial busters in your life to help you face your denial?

On page 43 of *Life's Healing Choices*, we find that Choice 2 is made up of three magnificent truths about God: *(1) He exists, (2) I matter to Him,* and *(3) He has the power to help me.* As we begin to understand each truth, we'll see that each one involves choices on our part—a choice to believe and a choice to receive. Unless we make these choices, His power cannot become real in our lives. Let's look at the truth about God.

GOD EXISTS

The Bible makes it clear that belief in God is essential: *"Anyone who comes to him must believe that he exists and that he rewards those who earnestly seek him"* (Hebrews 11:6 NIV).

+ What does this verse mean to you? What does it mean to *"earnestly seek him"*?

YOU MATTER TO HIM

Since most people believe God exists, the real issue becomes, "What kind of God is He? Do I really matter to Him?" This is how much God cares about us: *"God showed his great love for us by sending Christ to die for us"* (Romans 5:8 TLB).

+ Write down, maybe for the first time in your life, how much you matter to God!

GOD HAS THE POWER TO CHANGE YOU AND YOUR SITUATION

The magnitude of this power is hard to comprehend, so the apostle Paul prayed for our understanding: *"I pray that you will begin to understand the incredible greatness of his power for us who believe him. This is the same mighty power that raised Christ from the dead"* (Ephesians 1:19–20 NLT). The Bible goes on to say that *nothing* is too hard for God: *"What is impossible with men is possible with God"* (Luke 18:27 NIV).

+ What situation are you in right now that may seem hopeless? Write it down.

+ If you feel safe, share it with your group. If you are not ready to share it with your group as yet, share it with a safe person today! Write down the name of the person you will share it with.

STORIES OF
Changed Lives

Starting on page 55 of *Life's Healing Choices*, you will find Mary's and Tim's Stories of Changed Lives for Choice 2.

1. How did Mary's and Tim's misunderstanding of the Truth about God negatively affect each of their lives?

   + Mary:

   + Tim:

2. List some of the positive ways Mary's and Tim's lives changed when they were each able to make the second choice.

   + Mary:

   + Tim:

Important reminder: If you are still looking for a safe person with whom to start sharing your individual healing journey through the eight choices, you will find some helpful guidelines on pages 53–54 of *Life's Healing Choices* that will help you in your search.

Notes

FOR CHOICE 2

Prayer Requests
FOR WEEK 2

R
E

Consciously choose

O

to *commit* all my life and will

to Christ's care and control.

V

E

R

Y

"Happy are the meek."
MATTHEW 5:5 TEV/NIV

Letting GO

The COMMITMENT Choice

THE COMMITMENT CHOICE PRAYER

Dear God, I believe You sent Your Son, Jesus, to die for my sins so I can be forgiven. I'm sorry for my sins, and I want to live the rest of my life the way You want me to. Please put Your Spirit in my life to direct me. Amen.

LIFE'S
Healing Choices
SMALL GROUP STUDY

WEEK 3 ASSIGNMENTS

1. Read *Life's Healing Choices*—Choice 3 (pages 71–99).

2. Complete the *Small Group Study* questions for Choice 3. Be specific!

Important reminder: Please come to your small group prepared. That means completing both the reading and written assignments prior to your weekly meeting!

Choice 3

SMALL GROUP STUDY QUESTIONS

CYCLE OF DESPAIR

As we try to keep up a good front and convince ourselves that we have everything under control regarding our hurts, hang-ups, and habits, we become stuck in the "Cycle of Despair" (on page 72 of *Life's Healing Choices*). We start feeling *guilty* about our behavior. We wish we could get out of our mess, but we can't. After a lot of failed attempts, we get *angry* with ourselves and others: "I should be able to change. I ought to be able to get out of this." But we can't, and our anger grows. Over time, our anger turns to the *fear* that things are never going to change. We begin to realize that our hurts, hang-ups, and habits are controlling us, and our fear eventually turns to *depression*. We start feeling sorry for ourselves, and we become filled with yet more guilt.

39

+ Are you currently trapped in the cycle of despair? If so, where are you trapped? Be specific. Guilt, anger, fear, or depression? List some examples.

BREAKING THE CYCLE

When we finally realize we can't break this cycle on our own, we are ready to cross the line toward the "commitment choice," the one where we give all our hurts, hang-ups, and habits to God instead of trying to fix our problems ourselves. Jesus is reaching out to you, waiting for you to step across that line and into His open arms: *"Come to me, all of you who are weary and over-burdened, and I will give you rest! Put on my yoke and learn from me. For I am gentle and humble in heart and you will find rest for your souls. For my yoke is easy and my burden is light"* (Matthew 11:28–30 Phillips).

It has been said that our choices determine our circumstances and our decisions determine our destiny. There are five things that keep us from making this third choice: *pride, guilt, fear, worry,* and *doubt.*

+ How can each of these five things hold us back from making the decision to surrender our problems and our lives to the care and control of Christ?

+ Pride—

+ Guilt—

+ Fear—

+ Worry—

+ Doubt—

+ Which of these is holding you back? What is delaying your decision to surrender your problems and your life to the care and control of Christ?

On pages 81–82 of *Life's Healing Choices*, there are four steps that will help us make this third choice, help us *step across the line* and choose to commit our lives and wills to Christ's care and control. They are:

1. Accept God's Son as Your Savior

The Bible says, *"Believe in the Lord Jesus, and you will be saved"* (Acts 16:31 NIV).

+ What does this verse mean to you?

2. Accept God's Word as Your Standard

"All Scripture is inspired by God and is useful for teaching the faith and correcting error, for resetting the direction of a man's life and training him in good living" (2 Timothy 3:16 Phillips).

+ How can and do you use God's Word as the manual to guide your life?

3. Accept God's Will as Your Purpose

In Psalm 40:8 NCV, David says, *"My God, I want to do what you want. Your teachings are in my heart."*

+ List some specific actions you take to follow God's will and purpose for your life.

4. Accept God's Power as Your Strength

"I can do everything God asks me to with the help of Christ who gives me the strength and power" (Philippians 4:13 TLB).

+ What does this verse mean to you? In what area do you need God's strength today?

Starting on page 87 of *Life's Healing Choices,* you will find Lisa and Charlie's Stories of Changed Lives for Choice 3.

1. List some specific examples of how their lives were before they made the third choice.

    •   Lisa:

    •   Charlie:

2. List some specific examples of how Lisa's and Charlie's lives changed after they made the third choice and consciously chose to commit their lives and wills to Christ's care and control.

    •   Lisa:

+ Charlie:

Important reminder: Congratulations! If you prayed the Choice 3 prayer, on page 84 of *Life's Healing Choices* for the first time, welcome to God's family! Please do not feel you need to understand everything about the commitment you just made. Understanding will come as you grow and mature in your walk with Christ. For now, let these words be your comfort: Jesus says, *"Are you tired? Worn out? Burned out on religion? Come to me. Get away with me and you'll recover your life. I'll show you how to take a real rest. Walk with me and work with me—watch how I do it. Learn the unforced rhythms of grace. I won't lay anything heavy or ill-fitting on you. Keep company with me and you'll learn to live freely and lightly"* (Matthew 11:28 MSG).

There's more good news! *"What this means is that those who become Christians become new persons. They are not the same anymore, for the old life is gone. A new life has begun!"* (2 Corinthians 5:17 NLT). As you complete the remaining five choices, your life will never be the same. Your new life has begun!

If you have previously asked Christ into your heart, use this prayer time to commit to continually seek and follow His will for your life.

Notes

FOR CHOICE 3

Prayer Requests
FOR WEEK 3

R
E
C

Openly examine

and *confess* my faults to myself,

to God, and to someone I trust.

V
E
R
Y

"Happy are the pure in heart."
MATTHEW 5:8 TEV

Coming CLEAN

The HOUSECLEANING Choice

THE HOUSECLEANING CHOICE PRAYER

Dear God, You know my past—all the good and bad choices I have made and all the good and bad things I have done. In working through Choice 4, I ask that You give me the strength and courage to list the items called for below so that I can come clean and face the truth. Please open my eyes to the truth of my past—the truth of how others have hurt me and how I have hurt others. Please help me reach out to others You have placed along my pathway to healing. Thank You for providing these individuals to help me keep balanced as I do my inventory.
As I come clean in this choice, I thank You in advance for the forgiveness You have given me. In Christ's name I pray. Amen.

WEEK 4 ASSIGNMENTS

1. Read *Life's Healing Choices*—Choice 4 (pages 101–27).

2. Complete the Small Group Study questions for Choice 4. Be specific!

Important reminder: Please come to your small group prepared. That means completing both the reading and written assignments prior to your weekly meeting!

Go back to the *Life's Healing Choices* Small Group Covenant that you signed on page 7 that states: I will ask one member, of the same sex, in my group to be my accountability partner. Remember Ecclesiastes 4:9–10. If you have not yet asked someone in your group to be your accountability partner, it is very important that you do so this week before starting Choice 4.

Choice 4

SMALL GROUP STUDY QUESTIONS

Congratulations! You have covered Choices 1 through 3. Sometimes we get caught up in moving ahead, moving on to the next choice. It is important to take a few minutes and reflect on the progress that you have made thus far in your journey.

+ List the key insights that God has shown you in the first three choices.

+ How have you been changed by *Admitting Need, Getting Help,* and *Letting Go?*

   + Admitting Need:

+ Getting Help:

+ Letting Go:

OVERCOMING GUILT

If we are ever to recover from the hurts, hang-ups, and habits in our lives and know the joy of a pure heart, we'll have to learn how to let go of our guilt and shame and how to gain a clear conscience. The good news is by making Choice 4, you will find the key to relief from your guilt. If you take the steps needed to complete this choice, you will know the happiness of a *pure heart* as you share the words of the psalmist: "*What happiness for those whose guilt has been forgiven. What joys when sins are covered over! What relief for those who have confessed their sins and God has cleared their record*" (Psalm 32:1 TLB).

+ What does this verse mean to you? Especially focus on the words "happiness," "forgiven," and "confessed."

Before we start working on steps to overcoming guilt, it's important to understand the negative effects guilt has on our lives. *Guilt destroys our confidence, guilt damages our relationships, and guilt keeps us stuck in the past.*

+ List some specific examples from your life about how guilt has negatively affected you.

On pages 106–14 of *Life's Healing Choices*, there are five steps that will help you move past your guilt.

1. Take a Personal Moral Inventory

"Search me, O God, and know my heart; test my thoughts. Point out anything you find in me that makes you sad and lead me along the path of everlasting life" (Psalm 139:23–24 TLB).

+ How will taking a moral inventory help free me from my guilt?

Special note: It is important to keep our inventories *balanced.* When you do your personal moral inventory, it is very important to also list the "Good Choices" that you have made in your life. Our lives are shaped by a combination of the good and poor choices each of us has made. If we focus only on our poor choices our inventories will be distorted.

- Write down the top three "Good Choices" that you have made in your life.

    1.

    2.

    3.

2. Accept Responsibility for Your Faults

"The LORD gave us mind and conscience. We cannot hide from ourselves" (Proverbs 20:27 TEV).

+ How will accepting responsibility for my faults help free me from my guilt?

Special note: If you have been physically or sexually abused as a child or adult, I want you to know that I am sorry that you suffered through that abuse. There is no way I can know the pain it caused you, but I want you to know that I empathize with your hurt. When you start writing down your list of wrongs, simply put the words "NOT GUILTY" for the abuse that was done to you. *No part of that sin committed against you was your fault.* Renounce the lie that the abuse was your fault. However, accept responsibility for how you may have hurt others because of your reactions to your past abuse.

3. Ask God for Forgiveness

"No matter how deep the stain of your sins, I can take it out and make you as clean as freshly fallen snow" (Isaiah 1:18 TLB).

- How will asking God for forgiveness help free me from my guilt?

4. Admit Your Faults to Another Person

"Admit your faults to one another and pray for each other so that you may be healed" (James 5:16 TLB).

- How will admitting my faults to another person help free me from my guilt?

5. Accept God's Forgiveness and Forgive Yourself

"All have sinned and are not good enough for God's glory, and all need to be made right with God by his grace, which is a free gift. They need to be made free from sin through Jesus Christ" (Romans 3:23–24 NCV).

- How will accepting God's forgiveness and forgiving myself help free me from my guilt?

Starting on page 118 of *Life's Healing Choices*, you will find CJ and Linda's Story of Changed Lives for Choice 4.

1. List some specific examples of how CJ's and Linda's lives changed after they made the fourth choice to "Openly examine and confess my faults to myself, to God, and to someone I trust."

   ◆ CJ:

   ◆ Linda:

Important reminder: When you actually start working the three action steps for Choice 4, in the "Make the Choice" section of the book, you may experience a lot of pain and distress over completing your inventory. Writing down the events of your past may be just too difficult to do on your own, I understand. I suggest you go to www.celebraterecovery.com and find a Celebrate Recovery near you. There you will find help and support in completing your inventory. You will find people who have dealt with the same hurts, hang-ups, and habits that you are going through. You will find a safe place!

LIFE'S
Healing Choices
SMALL GROUP STUDY

Notes
FOR CHOICE 4

LIFE'S
Healing Choices
SMALL GROUP STUDY

Prayer Requests
FOR WEEK 4

R
E
C
O

Voluntarily submit

to every *change* God wants to make
in my life and humbly ask Him
to remove my character defects.

E
R
Y

"Happy are those whose greatest desire is to do what God requires."
MATTHEW 5:6 TEV

Making CHANGES

The TRANSFORMATION Choice

THE TRANSFORMATION CHOICE PRAYER

Dear God, thank You for Your forgiveness. Now I am ready and willing to submit to any and all changes You want to make in my life. By Your grace, I am ready to face it and deal with the defects one by one.

I have defects that have hurt me and defects that have hurt others. I've lived with some of these defects for so long that they have become a part of who I am. I have tried by my own power to fight against my defects and have failed over and over. I now ask by Your power and the power of Your Holy Spirit that You transform my mind, my heart, and my actions.

I need Your help in knowing where to start. I cannot handle all my defects at once. I can only face them one at a time. Show me, Lord, where should I begin? Help me as I look over my inventory list. Which character defect is the most damaging to my life? Where do I need to start? I am ready to follow Your lead. Amen.

Healing Choices
SMALL GROUP STUDY

WEEK 5 ASSIGNMENTS

1. Read *Life's Healing Choices*—Choice 5 (pages 129–64).

2. Complete the *Small Group Study* questions for Choice 5. Be specific!

Important reminder: Please come to your small group prepared. That means completing both the reading and written assignments prior to your weekly meeting!

Choice 5

SMALL GROUP STUDY QUESTIONS

The beatitude paired with this choice says,

"Happy are those whose greatest desire is to do what God requires."
MATTHEW 5:6 TEV

One of the things He requires is *change*, and that change begins with your submission to His power. Will the changes be easy? Will they happen overnight? Of course not. But the promise of this beatitude is that when your greatest desire is to do what God requires, you'll be *happy*.

You know God has forgiven you; now He wants to change you. He loves you too much to leave you the way you are.

In this choice we will learn how to *cooperate with God in His process of changing us*. But first, we'll look at the *origin of our character defects* and *why it is so hard for us to get rid of them*.

WHERE DO OUR CHARACTER DEFECTS COME FROM?

Our character defects come from three sources: biological, sociological, and theological. We'll examine these three sources through our *chromosomes*, our *circumstances*, and our *choices*.

1. Our Chromosomes

You inherited some of your parents' strengths and some of their weaknesses. You inherited many positive traits from them, but you also inherited some of their negative characteristics. You inherited some physical defects, as well as some emotional defects. This explains your predisposition toward certain problems.

List some of the positive and negative characteristics that you feel you have inherited from your parents.

+ Positive characteristics:

+ Negative characteristics:

2. Our Circumstances

The circumstances of how you were raised and what you saw as you grew up, even your current circumstances, contribute to your character. Much of how you behave and relate you learned from watching others. When you were very young, you learned from watching your parents. As you grew you learned from watching others—your peers, your teachers. You developed certain patterns and habits; many of them were attempts to protect yourself, to handle hurt and rejection, and to cope.

How have your circumstances, past and present, caused you to develop your character defects? Be specific.

3. Our Choices

The choices you make are the most significant source of your character defects, because they are the one thing you can do something about. You can't control or change who your parents are. You can't go back and change the environment of your childhood. But you can, with God's power, change the choices you make.

What are some of the specific choices that you have made that have led to you developing your defects of character?

WHY DOES IT TAKE SO LONG TO GET RID OF OUR CHARACTER DEFECTS?

Why is it so hard to change the defects in our lives? There are four main reasons: (1) because we've had them so long; (2) because we confuse our defects with our identity; (3) because every defect has a payoff; and (4) because Satan discourages our efforts to change.

Special note: The Bible says that Satan is a liar: *"There is no truth in him. When he tells a lie, he shows what he is really like, because he is a liar and the father of lies"* (John 8:44 NCV). But counteracting Satan's lies is the truth that sets us free. Jesus said, *"You will know the truth, and the truth will set you free"* (John 8:32 NIV). As you grow in God's truth and voluntarily submit to the changes He has in store for you, you will discover the happiness of doing what God requires.

+ Which of the above four main reasons is holding you back from making the changes God wants you to make in your life, and why?

HOW DO WE COOPERATE WITH GOD'S CHANGE PROCESS?

Go back to page 129 of *Life's Healing Choices* and read about the autopilot setting on the boat. The only way to change the direction of our lives—long-term—is to reset our autopilot. That's what the *transformation* choice is all about. Remember also the verse that says, *"Be transformed by the renewing of your* mind" (Romans 12:2 NIV). If we want to change our lives, we've got to reset the autopilot on the way we think. Our thoughts determine our feelings, and our feelings determine our actions.

Beginning on page 137 of *Life's Healing Choices* there are seven focus points that show you how to *cooperate* with God as He works to change your autopilot and gets you heading in the right direction.

1. Focus on Changing One Defect at a Time

"An intelligent person aims at wise action, but a fool starts off in many directions" (Proverbs 17:24 TEV).

- Write down the character defect that is causing you the most pain right now and why.

2. Focus on Victory One Day at a Time

"Don't be anxious about tomorrow. God will take care of your tomorrow too. Live one day at a time" (Matthew 6:34 TLB).

+ Why is it important to daily celebrate each victory you have over your defects of character?

3. Focus on God's Power, Not Your Willpower

"*I can do everything through him who gives me strength*" (Philippians 4:13 NIV).

+ How can storing this verse in your heart help you overcome your character defects?

4. Focus on the Good Things, Not the Bad

"*Fix your thoughts on what is true and good and right. Think about things that are pure. . . . Think about all you can praise God for and be glad about*" (Philippians 4:8 TLB).

+ What are some ways you can start focusing on the good, positive things in your life?

5. Focus on Doing Good, Not Feeling Good

"If you are guided by the Spirit you will be in no danger of yielding to self-indulgence" (Galatians 5:16 NJB). As we focus on doing what's right, we must draw on the power of the Holy Spirit, whom God has placed in all believers.

+ How will Galatians 5:16 help you do what is right?

6. Focus on People Who Help, Not Hinder You

"Do not be fooled: 'Bad friends will ruin good habits'" (1 Corinthians 15:33 NCV).

+ List some people who are not safe for you. These are the people who may hinder the positive choices that you are making.

+ List some people that will help you make good choices.

7. Focus on Progress, Not Perfection

"I am sure that God, who began the good work within you, will continue his work until it is finally finished on that day when Christ Jesus comes back again" (Philippians 1:6 NLT).

+ In the last five weeks, in what areas of your life have you noticed that you have been able to make better, Healing Choices? List them.

Starting on page 149 of *Life's Healing Choices*, you will find Dovey's and John's Stories of Changed Lives for Choice 5.

1. What were some defects of character that they needed to ask God for help to remove?

   + Dovey:

   + John:

2. What are some of the victories God gave Dovey and John over their defects of character? How did their lives change?

   + Dovey:

   + John:

Notes

FOR CHOICE 5

Prayer Requests
FOR WEEK 5

R
E
C
O
V
E
R
Y

Evaluate all my relationships.

Offer *forgiveness* to those who have hurt me, and make amends for harm I've done to others, except when to do so would harm them or others.

"*Happy are those who are merciful to others.*"
MATTHEW 5:7 TEV

"*Happy are those who work for peace.*"
MATTHEW 5:9 TEV

Repairing RELATIONSHIPS

The RELATIONSHIP Choice

THE RELATIONSHIP CHOICE PRAYER

Dear God, You have shown me that holding on to resentment for the wrongs done to me and refusing to make right my own wrongs has crippled me—emotionally, spiritually, and even physically. I ask You today to help me be honest about the hurts I feel. I've stuffed some and ignored others, but now I am ready to come clean and tell the truth about my pain. As I do, I ask that You give me the strength and the courage so I can release those who have hurt me and let go of my resentment toward them. Only by Your power will I be able to do this, Lord.

I pray, also, that You will give me the courage and discernment to know how to make amends to those I have hurt. Help me to be honest as I look back and remember, and guide me as I find the ways to make restitution, where appropriate.

Finally, I pray that I can begin a new life today as I refocus my life on doing Your will in my relationships. Help me set aside my selfishness and set my whole heart on You—I know I have a long way to go. I want the promise found in Job that all my troubles will fade from my memory and be remembered no more. Amen.

WEEK 6 ASSIGNMENTS

1. Read *Life's Healing Choices*—Choice 6 (pages 167–202).

2. Complete the *Small Group Study* questions for Choice 6. Be specific!

Important reminder: Please come to your *Life's Healing Choices* small group prepared. That means completing both the reading and written assignments prior to your weekly meeting!

Choice **6**

SMALL GROUP STUDY QUESTIONS

In this choice we'll work on making "corrections" in some of our relationships by doing some relational repair work. And we'll do that by working through a two-part process: We'll start off by *forgiving* those who have hurt us, and then we will work on *making amends* to those we have hurt.

When we are *merciful* to others, we are willing to forgive them, whether they deserve it or not. That's what mercy is about—it's undeserved. And when we *work for peace*, we put out real effort to make amends where we have wronged another, and we work to bring harmony back into that relationship.

We'll look back on our lives for the purpose of evaluating, not regretting. We'll learn how to repair the damage that others have done to us and that we have done to others.

Let's begin with forgiving others for the wrongs they have done against us. But *why* should you do this and *how* do you do it?

WHY SHOULD YOU FORGIVE OTHERS?

There are at least three reasons, and believe it or not, the benefits are all yours.

1. Because God Has Forgiven You

"*You must make allowance for each other's faults and forgive the* person who offends you. Remember, the Lord forgave you, so you must forgive others" (Colossians 3:13 NLT). If God has forgiven you, shouldn't you forgive others?

+ How will this verse help you to start the process of forgiving those who have hurt you?

2. Because Resentment Doesn't Work

The second reason you need to forgive those who have hurt you is purely practical: resentment doesn't work. Holding on to resentment is unreasonable and unhelpful. "*To worry yourself to death with resentment would be a foolish, senseless thing to do*" (Job 5:2 TEV).

+ Why is holding on to your resentments foolish and senseless?

Resentment is also *unhealthy*. *"Some people stay healthy till the day they die. . . . Others have no happiness at all; they live and die with bitter hearts"* (Job 21:23, 25 TEV). Resentment is like a cancer that eats you alive. It's an emotional poison with physical consequences.

+ How has holding on to your resentments affected you physically and emotionally?

3. Because You'll Need Forgiveness in the Future

The Bible says you cannot receive what you are unwilling to give: *"Forgive us our debts, as we forgive our debtors"* (Matthew 6:12 KJV).

+ How will this verse help encourage you in giving your forgiveness to others? And why is it so important?

FORGIVING OTHERS

Forgiving others is not easy. How do you forgive those who have hurt you? The "Three Rs," *Reveal, Release,* and *Replace,* can show you how.

+ How can *Revealing Your Hurt, Releasing Your Offender,* and *Replacing Your Hurt with God's Peace* help you to forgive others?

    + Revealing Your Hurt:

    + Releasing Your Offender:

    + Replacing Your Hurt with God's Peace:

Special note: Is it always wise or safe to release the offender face-to-face? Not always. And in some cases it's not even possible to go back to the people who have hurt you. You may not be able to find them. They may have remarried, moved away, or even died. You may have been physically or sexually abused by someone. It still may not be safe to offer your forgiveness to them directly. You may run the risk of being hurt or abused by them again. Refer to page 174 in *Life's Healing Choices* to find two techniques you can use in cases like these.

+ List two people who you need to offer your forgiveness to and why.

MAKING AMENDS

Repairing relationships is a two-part process. In the first three questions we focused on *forgiveness;* the second part is *making amends.* Not only have people hurt you; you have hurt other people.

Why do we need to make amends and how do we do it? *"If you are standing before the altar in the Temple, offering a sacrifice to God, and you suddenly remember that someone has something against you, leave your sacrifice there beside the altar. Go and be reconciled to that person. Then come and offer your sacrifice to God"* (Matthew 5:23–24 NLT).

+ How does this verse help you see the importance of making amends to those you have hurt?

+ How will the following three actions help you make amends?

  + Making a list of those you've harmed and what you did:

+ Thinking about how you'd like someone to make amends to you:

+ Refocusing your life on doing God's will:

+ List two people you need to make amends to, and why.

Look at Carl's and Bill's stories beginning on page 187 of *Life's Healing Choices*. They both made the choices to offer forgiveness to those who hurt them and made their amends to those they hurt.

1. How did these choices free them from resentment and guilt?

   • Carl:

   • Bill:

Special note: When you actually start working the "Make the Choice" sections of *Life's Healing Choices,* it is very important that you share your Forgiveness List with your accountability partner prior to sharing it with the person who hurt you. Your accountability partner can help you develop a plan for safely offering your forgiveness to those on your list. Your accountability partner also knows you and can challenge you to include anyone you may have omitted.

Likewise, be sure to also share your Amends List with your accountability partner. An objective opinion can ensure that you make amends with the right motives. The Bible encourages us to *"consider how we may spur one another on toward love and good deeds"* (Hebrews 10:24 NIV). Just as your accountability partner helped you offer your forgiveness, he or she can help you plan the right time and place to make your amends. For example, if you owe someone money, your partner can help you develop restitution plans.

Once you have completed offering forgiveness and making amends, there will be no skeletons in your closet. You will have come to the point in your life where you can say, "I have nothing more to hide. I'm not perfect, I have attempted to repair all the harmful things I've done in my past. I have made amends and offered restitution for my part."

Notes
FOR CHOICE 6

LIFE'S
Healing Choices
SMALL GROUP STUDY

Prayer Requests
FOR WEEK 6

R

E

C

O

V

E

R

Y

Reserve a daily quiet time with God

for self-examination, Bible reading, and prayer
in order *to know* God and His will for my
life and to gain the power to follow His will.

Maintaining MOMENTUM

The GROWTH Choice

THE GROWTH CHOICE PRAYER

Special note: Praying the Scripture may be another new experience for you, but it's a prayer method that brings amazing blessings. In this action step, we'll pray through the Lord's Prayer. You will see how the eight choices support this great prayer. Even though you haven't yet come to chapter 8, you'll be able to pray this choice, too. As we pray, we'll focus our prayer to avoid the dangers of relapse.

Scripture: "*Our Father in heaven, hallowed be your name . . .*"
Choice 1: Realize I am not God . . .
Choice 2: Earnestly believe that God exists . . .
Prayer: Father in heaven, Your name is wonderful and holy. I acknowledge that You hold all power—that You are God and that on my own I am powerless. Without You, I will most certainly relapse into my old hurts, hang-ups, and habits.

Scripture: "*Your kingdom come . . .*"

Choice 8: Yield myself to God to be used . . .

Prayer: *I pray that Your kingdom will come in my life—that I will yield myself to be used by You, that You can use me to reach out to others with the Good News of Your kingdom and Your healing. Help me to find ways to serve You and others.*

Scripture: "*Your will be done on earth as it is in heaven . . .*"

Choice 5: Voluntarily submit to God's changes . . .

Prayer: *Oh, Lord, I pray that Your will be done in my life. I fight against it so often, but in my heart of hearts, I choose to submit to You. Help me to hold on to that choice. I choose Your will over my willpower; help me to not fall back into old patterns.*

Scripture: "*Give us today our daily bread . . .*"

Choice 3: Consciously choose to commit . . . to Christ's care . . .

Prayer: *Supply me with just what I need for today. Help me to take my recovery one day at a time, not looking too far ahead, but committing all my life and will to Christ's care and control—one day at a time.*

Scripture: "*Forgive us our debts . . .*"

Choice 4: Openly examine and confess my faults . . .

Prayer: *Forgive me, Lord. I have looked at my life and my heart, and what I've seen is not pretty. You already knew that, and I thank You for loving me anyway and for forgiving me so freely. Thank You for the loving support from others that You have provided along my healing journey.*

Scripture: *"As we also have forgiven our debtors . . ."*

Choice 6: Evaluate all my relationships . . .

Prayer: *Soften my heart toward those who have harmed me. Teach me, by Your power, to forgive, as You have forgiven me. And give me the courage, the conviction, and the wisdom to make amends where I have harmed others. Help me not to relapse into old patterns of resentment and bitterness.*

Scripture: *"And lead us not into temptation, but deliver us from the evil one . . ."*

Choice 7: Reserve a daily time with God . . .

Prayer: *Help me to spend time with You daily. I know that time with You is my best defense against relapse and my best offense toward growth. May my time with You create a hedge of protection around me. Amen.*

WEEK 7 ASSIGNMENTS

1. Read *Life's Healing Choices*—Choice 7 (pages 205–39).

2. Complete the *Small Group Study* questions for Choice 7. Be specific!

Important reminder: Please come to your small group prepared. That means completing both the reading and written assignments prior to your weekly meeting!

Choice 7

SMALL GROUP STUDY QUESTIONS

This week we're going to focus on helping you maintain your momentum. The fact is, growth is not smooth. The road to healing is bumpy. Some days it's two steps forward and one step back. Just because you are completing this curriculum and attempting to start to live out these biblical choices does not mean your journey will be problem free.

If you don't keep your guard up, you can easily fall back into your old self-defeating patterns. This is called *relapse*. We all tend to repeat the patterns of our past. It's easy to slip back into old hurts, old hang-ups, and old habits.

This week, we'll begin to understand relapse—its *patterns* and *causes*. Then we'll learn how to *prevent* relapse in the first place.

PATTERN OF RELAPSE

Let's first look at the very predictable pattern of relapse. Regardless of the issue, the pattern is usually the same.

+ Write down your understanding of each of the following four components in the relapse pattern, then write down how each of them could lead you to relapse if you are not daily maintaining the momentum of Choice 7.

- Complacency—

- Confusion—

- Compromise—

- Catastrophe—

CAUSES OF RELAPSE

Why do we fall into the predictable pattern of relapse when we know which way to go; when we know the right thing to do?

Why do we tend to ignore what we know is right? There are four things that can cause us to relapse.

1. We Revert to Our Own Willpower

"How can you be so foolish! You began by God's Spirit; do you now want to finish by your own power?" (Galatians 3:3 TEV).

+ How can this verse keep you from reverting back to your own willpower?

2. We Ignore One of the Choices

"You were doing so well! Who made you stop obeying the truth?" (Galatians 5:7 TEV). The truth is that we need to follow through on all the choices, or the plan doesn't work. It's been tried and proven countless times over.

+ How can skipping or not completing one of the choices lead you to relapse?

3. We Try to Recover without Support

"Two people are better than one, because they get more done by working together. If one falls down, the other can help him up. But it is bad for the person who is alone and falls, because no one is there to help" (Ecclesiastes 4:9–10 NCV).

+ List some ways in which having someone to hold you accountable will help you from relapsing.

4. We Become Prideful

"Pride goes before destruction" (Proverbs 16:18 TLB). The secret to lasting recovery is to live in humility: *"Humble yourselves before the Lord, and he will lift you up"* (James 4:10 NIV).

+ List some ways why humility is the best protection against relapse.

PREVENTING RELAPSE

The keys to preventing relapse are found in the words of Choice 7:

Reserve a daily quiet time with God for self-examination, Bible reading, and prayer in order to know God and His will for my life and to gain the power to follow His will.

We need to develop new habits. New healthy habits are about making daily choices that put us in a place where God can begin His transformation work in us. Let's look at three healthy habits that will help us prevent relapse.

Habit 1: Evaluation

The Bible makes it clear that we are to evaluate ourselves: *"Let's take a good look at the way we're living and reorder our lives under God"* (Lamentations 3:40 MSG).

What you should evaluate

1. *Physical:* Write down, "What is my body telling me right now? Am I hungry? Am I tired? Am I fatigued? Am I stressed out?"

2. *Emotional:* Write down, "What am I feeling right now? What are my positive and negative feelings?"

Special note: Repressing your real feelings is like shaking up a bottle of Coke and not taking the cap off; it's going to blow eventually. You need to take time for a "Heart Check." Do this check frequently and respond to your emotional needs.

H – am I *h*urting?

E – am I *e*xhausted?

A – am I *a*ngry?

R – do I *r*esent anybody?

T – am I *t*ense?

3. *Relational:* Answer these questions:

+ Am I at peace with everyone? If not, why?

+ Am I holding on to a new hurt? Who hurt me and how did they hurt me?

+ Have I recently hurt someone and not made amends? Who have I hurt? How and why did I hurt them?

4. *Spiritual:* Answer these questions:

+ How am I doing in my relationship with God today?

+ Did I spend time alone with God today? If not, why? If I did, what did He show me today?

- How am I learning to rely on Him day by day, moment by moment?

When you should evaluate

There are three kinds of evaluations that we need to do: a *spot-check evaluation,* a *daily review,* and an *annual checkup.*

- Why is each important in order for you to maintain momentum in Choice 7?

  - Spot-check evaluation:

  - Daily review:

+ Annual checkup:

Habit 2: Meditation

"They delight in doing everything God wants them to, and day and night are always meditating on his laws and thinking about ways to follow him more closely. They are like trees along a riverbank bearing luscious fruit each season without fail. Their leaves shall never wither, and all they do shall prosper" (Psalm 1:2–3 TLB). Meditation may be a new concept to you, but it really isn't all that hard.

+ What are some of the blessings that you can or have received from God through meditation?

Having God's Word in your heart is a powerful deterrent to sin and relapse. *"I have thought much about your words and stored them in my heart so that they would hold me back from sin"* (Psalm 119:11 TLB).

+ How do you store God's words in your heart?

Habit 3: Prayer

Pray about anything! Prayer is your way of plugging into God's power. You pray, "God, I can't do it, but You can." Jesus said to *"watch and pray so that you will not fall into temptation"* (Mark 14:38 NIV). You can take any need, any struggle, to God.

+ How can prayer help you maintain your momentum and help prevent you from relapsing?

+ List specific examples of how God has answered your prayers over the last seven weeks.

Look at Regina's and Steve's stories starting on page 224 of *Life's Healing Choices.*

1. How did their relapses hurt their lives and others'?

    + Regina:

    + Steve:

2. How did working Choice 7 daily help them stop relapsing and help change their lives?

    + Regina:

    + Steve:

Notes
FOR CHOICE 7

Prayer Requests
FOR WEEK 7

R
E
C
O
V
E
R

"*Happy are those who are persecuted because they do what God requires.*"
MATTHEW 5:10 TEV

Yield myself to God

to be *used* to bring this Good News to others,
both by my example and by my words.

Recycling PAIN

The SHARING Choice

THE SHARING CHOICE PRAYER

Dear God, help me be ready to share with someone today the victories You have given me. Help me find the right words and the right time to share my heart with someone who is hurting and doesn't know where to go or how to stop the pain. I pray that I can share the ways you freed me from my hurts, hangups, and habits. Let me do so with gentleness and respect. Thank You for letting me serve You today in this way. Amen.

WEEK 8 ASSIGNMENTS

1. Read *Life's Healing Choices*—Choice 8 (pages 241–67).

2. Complete the *Small Group Study* questions for Choice 8. Be specific!

Important reminder: Please come to your small group prepared. That means completing both the reading and written assignments prior to your weekly meeting!

Choice 8

SMALL GROUP STUDY QUESTIONS

In this, the last chapter and the last choice, we'll see that the "Y" in R-E-C-O-V-E-R-Y stands for *yield*. It also stands for *you*. God wants *you* to yield to Him and allow Him to recycle the pain in your life for the benefit of others.

"*'My gracious favor is all you need. My power works best in your weakness.' So now I am glad to boast about my weaknesses, so that the power of Christ may work through me*" (2 Corinthians 12:9 NLT). People are not helped by our strengths; they're helped when we're honest about our weaknesses. When you understand that God uses your weaknesses and your pain, life takes on a whole new meaning and you experience genuine recovery. The proof that you are truly recovering is when you begin to focus outside yourself, when you stop being absorbed with *your* needs, *your* hurts, *your* problems. Recovery is evident when you begin to say, "How can I help others?"

In this final week, we'll answer two important questions: Why does God allow our pain? and, How can we use our pain to help others?

WHY DOES GOD ALLOW PAIN?

Why God allows pain and suffering is a universal question. There are several reasons, but here we'll share about the big four.

1. God Has Given Us a Free Will

God created us with the right to choose. In the Book of Beginnings, Genesis 1:27 NIV, we read, *"God created man in his own image."*

+ Describe in your own words how your free will is not only a blessing but a burden.

2. God Uses Pain to Get Our Attention

"Sometimes it takes a painful experience to make us change our ways" (Proverbs 20:30 TEV).

+ Describe how God has used pain in your life as a wake-up call.

3. God Uses Pain to Teach Us to Depend on Him

"We were really crushed and overwhelmed ... [and] saw how powerless we were to help ourselves; but that was good, for then we

put everything into the hands of God, who alone could save us" (2 Corinthians 1:8–9 TLB).

+ What are some of the things God has taught you through your pain?

4. God Allows Pain to Give Us a Ministry to Others

When we turn to God for healing from the source of our pain, He comforts us and gives us the help we need. "*Why does he [God] do this? So that when others are troubled, needing our sympathy and encouragement, we can pass on to them this same help and comfort God has given us*" (2 Corinthians 1:4 TLB).

+ How does pain actually make you humble, sympathetic, and sensitive to others' needs?

+ How does your pain prepare you to serve others?

HOW CAN WE USE OUR PAIN TO HELP OTHERS?

Let's focus on the three ways you can use your pain to help others.

1. Accept Your Mission

God has a mission for you. It's called the Great Commission, and it's found in the Bible: *"Go and make disciples of all the nations, baptizing them in the name of the Father and the Son and the Holy Spirit"* (Matthew 28:19 NLT).

+ What does the Great Commission mean to you?

+ How can you do your part?

2. Tell Your Story

+ How will being humble, being real, and not lecturing help you prepare to share your story?

3. Consider Your Beneficiaries

+ How would others benefit from hearing your story?

+ Who could best benefit from hearing your story?

Look at Tina's and Bob's stories beginning on page 253 of *Life's Healing Choices.*

1. List the pain that they went through.

   • Tina:

   • Bob:

2. How has God used Tina's and Bob's pain to help others?

3. How did their stories help you?

Special note: As you come to the end of your eight weeks, it is important to allow time for closure for your group. Please spend the remaining twenty minutes sharing the next two questions.

+ Over the past eight weeks, what are the two most important things God has shown you about your life and the choices you have made?

+ What is the next action that you are going to take to find further freedom from your life's hurts, hang-ups, and habits?

Special note: For some suggestions, turn to the next page. You will find three "Next Steps" to choose from that will help you continue your healing journey.

WHERE DO *You* GO FROM HERE? 🍃

Congratulations on completing your *Life's Healing Choices Small Group Study*! Here are three suggested "Next Steps" to choose from.

STEP 1

If you have not already begun to work on the "Make the Choice" section at the end of each chapter of *Life's Healing Choices*, I encourage you to start now. This is where you will actually begin to experience the healing and victory God has planned for you over your hurts, hang-ups, and habits! There is a *Life's Healing Choices Guided Journal* that will help you create a written account of your progress as you complete each choice.

If after completing *Life's Healing Choices* Small Group Study, you have found that your hurts, hang-ups, and habits are deep and are really affecting your life and relationships, I encourage you to start attending a Celebrate Recovery group at a church near you.

You can find a Celebrate Recovery group in a church close to you by going to www.celebraterecovery.com. You will find men and women there who have gone through the same issues and struggles that you are facing. It is a safe place for you to find help, support, and victory over your life's hurts, hang-ups, and habits!

STEP 2

Start a daily habit, a positive habit, of getting into God's Word!

If you do not have a Bible, I suggest that you get the Celebrate Recovery Bible. It contains hundreds of additional pages that will give you a deeper insight into each of the eight choices.

STEP 3

I encourage you to start a new *Life's Healing Choices* small group.

Invite your friends, coworkers, neighbors, and/or family members to join. Help facilitate the group so that they can start to learn how they can find healing and victory over their life's hurts, hang-ups, and habits. This is part of living out the eighth choice.

Thank you for beginning this exciting journey with me. You are in my prayers.

To God be the glory!

John Baker

Notes
FOR CHOICE 8

Prayer Requests
FOR WEEK 8

HOW TO FACILITATE A *LIFE'S HEALING CHOICES* SMALL GROUP

Notes FOR SMALL GROUP FACILITATORS

Thank you for facilitating your *Life's Healing Choices* small group. The following are some proven suggestions that will help you facilitate your new group.

Prior to Your First Meeting

+ Read through this entire list of suggestions.

+ Be sure to contact all of your small group members a week prior to your first meeting. Welcome them and let them know that they should have week one of the *Life's Healing Choices* Small Group Study's assignments, on page 12, completed for the first meeting.

First Meeting—Week 1

+ At the beginning of your first meeting, read the *Life's Healing Choices* Small Group Covenant on page 7. You and each member of your small group should sign the Covenant prior to starting the first lesson.

+ If you have an existing small group that is made up of men and women for the next eight weeks, simply have the men meet in one room and the women meet in another. This will greatly increase the level of sharing.

At Every Meeting—Weeks 1 through 8

+ The small group should last between 1½ and 2 hours.

+ Each meeting should open and close in prayer.

+ The *Life's Healing Choices* Small Group Guidelines, on page 3, should be read by you at the beginning of each meeting.

Helpful Suggestions

+ Relax and enjoy your group. Your role is to facilitate, to ensure that the group runs smoothly. You are there to work on your own hurts, hang-ups, and habits. Your role is not to be a counselor. That is why the third guideline is so important: *"We are here to support one another. We will not attempt to fix one another."*

+ It is important to close your group to new members after the second week. This will ensure that all of the members feel safe as they share their lives' hurts, hang-ups, and habits.

+ Depending on the size of your group, you may not have enough time for all members to share their answers to every question in a particular lesson. They can share them with their accountability partner prior to the next meeting. The suggested group size is from six to twelve participants.

+ If an individual does not want to share his or her answer to a particular question with the group, let him or her know that it is okay. Encourage the person to share it with his or her accountability partner some time after the meeting.

+ Make sure to leave five to ten minutes at the end of each meeting for your group to share their prayer requests.

Also Available by John Baker

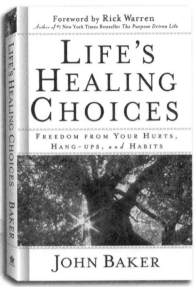

Foreword by Rick Warren
Author of #1 New York Times Bestseller The Purpose Driven Life

LIFE'S HEALING CHOICES

FREEDOM FROM YOUR HURTS,
HANG-UPS, *and* HABITS

JOHN BAKER

LIFE'S HEALING CHOICES
GUIDED JOURNAL

FREEDOM FROM YOUR HURTS, HANG-UPS, *and* HABITS

JOHN BAKER

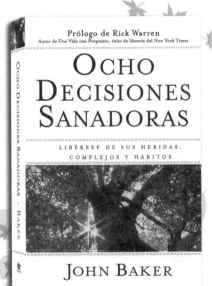

Prólogo de Rick Warren
Autor de Una Vida con Propósito, éxito de librería del New York Times

OCHO DECISIONES SANADORAS

LIBÉRESE DE SUS HERIDAS,
COMPLEJOS Y HÁBITOS

JOHN BAKER

Life's Healing Choices (Spanish)

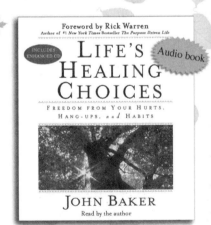

INCLUDES ENHANCED CD

Foreword by Rick Warren
Author of #1 New York Times Bestseller The Purpose Driven Life

LIFE'S HEALING CHOICES

Audio book

FREEDOM FROM YOUR HURTS,
HANG-UPS, *and* HABITS

JOHN BAKER
Read by the author

HOWARD BOOKS
A DIVISION OF SIMON & SCHUSTER